A TRUE BOOK™

NATURAL DISASTER!

# All About Wildfires

## Discovering How They Spark, Burn, and Spread

Alessandra Potenza

Children's Press®
An imprint of Scholastic Inc.

**Content Consultant**
Dr. Kristen Rasmussen
Assistant Professor
Department of Atmospheric Science
Colorado State University

Library of Congress Cataloging-in-Publication Data
Names: Potenza, Alessandra, author.
Title: All about wildfires / Alessandra Potenza.
Description: First edition. | New York : Children's Press, an imprint of Scholastic Inc. 2021. | Series: A true book: natural disaster! |Includes bibliographical references and index. | Audience: Ages 8–10. | Audience: Grades 4–6. | Summary: "This book shows readers the awesome power of wildfires"—Provided by publisher.
Identifiers: LCCN 2021003956 (print) | LCCN 2021003957 (ebook) | ISBN 9781338769531 (library binding) | ISBN 9781338769548 (paperback) | ISBN 9781338769555 (ebook)
Subjects: LCSH: Wildfires—Juvenile literature. | Wildfires—Prevention and control—Juvenile literature. | Fire extinction—Juvenile literature. | Climatic changes—Juvenile literature.
Classification: LCC SD421.23 .P674 2021  (print) | LCC SD421.23  (ebook) | DDC 634.9/618—dc23
LC record available at https://lccn.loc.gov/2021003956
LC ebook record available at https://lccn.loc.gov/2021003957

The publisher does not have any control over and does not assume any responsibility for author or third-party websites or their content.

10 9 8 7 6 5 4 3 2 1                                22 23 24 25 26

Printed in the U.S.A. 113
First edition, 2022

Series produced by Priyanka Lamichhane
Book design by Kathleen Petelinsek
Illustrations on pages 42–43 by Gary LaCoste

**Front cover: Background: A wildfire burns through a forest; inset photo, top: A smokejumper jumps out of a plane; inset top right: An airplane releases special chemicals over a wildfire to help stop its spread; inset, bottom left: A campfire burns in an open area, away from trees.**

**Back cover: A firefighter tackles a fast-moving wildfire.**

# Find the Truth!

**Everything** you are about to read is true *except* for one of the sentences on this page.

Which one is **TRUE**?

**T or F**   Some tree species need wildfires to survive.

**T or F**   Most wildfires in the United States are caused by lightning.

Find the answers in this book.

# What's in This Book?

The **BIG** Truth

Bark beetles like
this one destroy
dry trees.

# 3 Fighting Fire

# 4 Wildfire Safety

A smokejumper glides down to the ground after jumping from an airplane.

# Up in Smoke

Hot **embers** blanket the forest floor. Bright yellow and **orange flames** lick tree trunks and leaves. The hazy sky is **glowing red**. Soon, the whole forest is ablaze! This inferno is known as a wildfire, an unplanned fire that burns through a wilderness area.

These natural disasters happen all over the world. Every year in the United States, thousands of wildfires **burn through about 7 million acres** (2.8 million hectares) of land. That's an area slightly smaller than the state of Maryland. As wildfires spread, they destroy everything in their path, including **entire towns**.

Let's explore the science behind wildfires, how firefighters tame the flames, and what you can do to keep safe.

Wildfires are usually named after the location where they start.

A wildfire in California as seen from a satellite in space.

# Into the Flames

Wildfires can burn through many different types of natural areas, from forests to grasslands. Most wildfires are small and contained. But even a small wildfire can be dangerous. Flames can reach temperatures of about 1,472 degrees Fahrenheit (800 degrees Celsius) and travel up to 14 miles per hour (22 kilometers per hour). That may seem slow. But it's fast enough to endanger people and property. But how do wildfires start? And why are they so destructive?

## How Wildfires Happen

Some wildfires are caused naturally by lightning or volcanic eruptions. But most wildfires are caused by human activity. Sometimes, wildfires are started by accident—such as a spark from a campfire. Other times, people start wildfires to cause harm. This is called **arson**. In some countries, people set fire to forests on purpose in order to clear the land for farming. If these fires are not properly controlled, they can spread.

# The Fire Triangle

Like all fires, wildfires need three elements to burn: heat, fuel, and oxygen. This is called the fire triangle. A heat source is anything that will spark a fire, such as a lightning strike or a hot ember from a campfire. Fuel is anything that will catch fire, such as dead trees and logs. And finally, wildfires burn by consuming oxygen in the air. If you take away any of these elements, the fire will go out.

A spark from lightning, a dry tree, and wind create the fire triangle, the perfect conditions for a wildfire.

# Flames, Smoke, and Mud

Wildfires are dangerous for many reasons. As they burn vegetation, flames can also destroy buildings and kill people. Smoke from wildfires contains particles from burned-down materials that can make breathing difficult, especially for people with health conditions such as asthma. Wildfires can also increase the risk of **landslides**. Plant roots hold soil together. When plants burn, their roots are destroyed. When it rains, the soil can come loose, resulting in a landslide.

Children in Indonesia walk to school surrounded by the haze from a wildfire.

A car is stuck in a mudslide that happened after heavy rainfall in Turkey.

Fire tornadoes are also called fire whirls or firenadoes.

A home is in danger as a fire tornado spins near a southern California neighborhood.

# Fiery Tornadoes

Some wildfires are so large that they create their own weather. As hot air from wildfires rises quickly, more air rushes in to fill the space. This causes powerful winds. Sometimes, fire tornadoes form! They occur when intensely hot air from the fire spins as it rises. The whirl of air sucks in burning debris, ash, and hot gases, creating a fiery column shooting into the sky.

# Wildlife in Wildfires

When wildfires happen, humans are not the only ones affected. Animals may be in danger, too. Typically, animals can escape wildfires by flying or running away. Other animals hide underground or under rocks. But if wildfires are strong, animals may get hurt or die. Thankfully, officials and volunteers rush in to help! Zookeepers at the Australia Zoo rescued thousands of animals injured by severe wildfires that burned from summer 2019 until May 2020.

Koalas in Australia usually curl into a ball at the top of trees to escape flames.

A firefighter rescues a koala after wildfires sweep through a forest in Australia.

Veterinarians apply fish skin on a kitten after he has been burned.

Tilapia skin

# Fish-Skin Bandages!

In recent years, veterinarians have developed an unusual treatment for animals that get burns during wildfires: fish skin! The skin from tilapia is first thoroughly cleaned. Then it's applied on burned skin like a bandage. The fish skin contains a substance called collagen, which helps heal wounds. The treatment has been used on cats, dogs, bears, and mountain lions. A recent patient in California was a Boston terrier mix named Olivia.

This kitten's paws are bandaged after being treated with fish skin to help heal burns.

Olivia gets a hug after receiving her fish-skin bandages.

Wildfire smoke can travel thousands of miles. In the United States, smoke from the West Coast can make skies hazy on the East Coast.

Sunlight bouncing off ash and smoke particles from wildfires cause the sky above San Francisco to glow orange.

# Feeling the Heat

Wildfires around the world are becoming larger and more destructive. Scientists say that **climate change** is partly to blame. Climate change refers to the change in Earth's temperature and weather patterns over time. In the past few decades, the planet has become warmer. Extreme weather events are becoming more common. But why is climate change happening, and why does a warmer planet lead to more devastating wildfires? Let's find out.

# A Warming Planet

Climate change is happening because we burn **fossil fuels** for energy to run our cars, factories, and power plants. Fossil fuels include oil, coal, and natural gas. When these fuels burn, they release **greenhouse gases** into the air. These gases trap heat in Earth's **atmosphere**, causing the planet to warm up. This process is called the greenhouse effect.

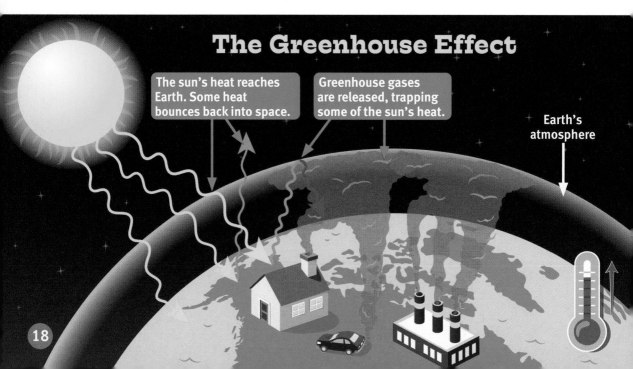

## The Greenhouse Effect

The sun's heat reaches Earth. Some heat bounces back into space.

Greenhouse gases are released, trapping some of the sun's heat.

Earth's atmosphere

Dry grass covers the landscape as firefighters try to put out a wildfire in Montana.

## Parched

Why does a warmer planet mean bigger wildfires? Warm temperatures dry out trees and shrubs. Because of rising temperatures, snow melts more quickly than it used to. This leads to drier soil and plants. **Droughts**, periods with little or no rain, are also becoming more frequent. When vegetation is dry, it catches fire more easily. Dry plants can also die. Dead vegetation litters landscapes with materials that burn easily.

A bark beetle is about as big as a cooked grain of rice.

Bark beetle

In Germany, a tree infested by bark beetles is marked with red paint so it can be taken down.

## Pesky Bugs

When a tree is dried out, it is more likely to become infested with insects such as bark beetles. These bugs drink tree sap, which causes trees to die. Warmer temperatures due to climate change also allow bark beetles to thrive and move to areas where they don't usually live. In recent years, the insects have killed millions of trees in the United States. Dead trees are the perfect fuel for wildfires.

# Near Nature

Climate change is not the only thing increasing the risk of destructive wildfires. Development of homes and communities is also contributing to the problem. More people in the United States are building new communities close to wilderness areas. This puts them and their property at higher risk of being affected by wildfires. Since 1990, more than 30 million new homes were built in and around forests, grasslands, and other natural areas.

A neighborhood of houses sits near a forested hillside in Utah.

# Are Some Wildfires Good?

Though wildfires can be destructive, they can also play an important role in nature. In fact, wildfires help keep **ecosystems** healthy! Some species of plants and animals even need fire to survive. Here are three benefits of wildfires.

**Reproduction:** Some species of trees, such as lodgepole pines and giant sequoias, depend on fire to reproduce. Heat from wildfires cracks open their cones, releasing seeds onto the forest floor. There, the seeds can grow into new trees.

## Room for sunlight:

In a thick forest, little sunlight reaches the forest floor. If too many dead leaves and branches cover the soil underneath trees, sunlight gets blocked. Wildfires help thin out the upper level of a forest, called the forest canopy. This allows more sunlight to reach the soil. New plants need that sunlight to grow.

## Provide nutrients:

The forest floor is littered with dry leaves, logs, and branches from dead plants. Wildfires quickly burn all that material into ash filled with nutrients. Seeds use those nutrients to grow into new plants.

23

From 2015 to 2019, about 88 percent of wildfires were caused by humans.

A firefighter struggles to stop a wildfire from burning down a house.

# Fighting Fire

Wildfires can be scary, but adults work hard to prevent wildfires from starting in the first place. If a wildfire does start, firefighters use special equipment and techniques to put out the flames. Some scientists even create fires in their labs to study flames under safe conditions. This helps them learn how to keep people and property safe.

# Preventing Wildfires

Remember the fire triangle? One element wildfires need in order to start is fuel such as dead, dried vegetation on a forest floor. To prevent wildfires, firefighters try to get rid of this fuel. How? By setting it on fire! It may seem odd to fight fire with fire. But that's exactly what firefighters do. These are called controlled fires, and they're done very carefully so the fire is contained and not dangerous.

A firefighter in Alberta, Canada, starts a controlled fire in order to get rid of dried grass.

# Ancient Use of Fire

Today, controlled fires are started routinely across U.S. forests. The idea isn't new. For thousands of years, Indigenous Peoples used small fires to remove dead vegetation and promote the growth of certain plants used for food, medicine, and to make baskets. The practice is part of their culture. But by the early 1900s, the U.S. government outlawed it. This allowed forests to become overgrown, increasing the risk of wildfires. Today, some Indigenous Peoples are working with scientists and officials to manage controlled fires. Here, Harold Myers (left) of the Yurok Tribe and Christopher Villarruel (right) of the Pit River Tribe start a controlled fire in Northern Califorina.

# Battling Blazes

If a wildfire does start, firefighters battle blazes with many tools. One is the Pulaski—a special axe with a flat blade. Crews use this tool and others, such as shovels and chain saws, to clear out vegetation in an area around a wildfire. These fire lines act as barriers that keep wildfires from spreading. To stay safe, firefighters wear special fire-resistant clothing that protects them from burns.

## Timeline of Firefighting in the United States

**1871**
The United States' deadliest wildfire, known as the Peshtigo Fire, burns more than 1.2 million acres of land and kills 1,182 people in Wisconsin.

**1886**
The first team of paid wildland firefighters is established in Yellowstone National Park.

**1911**
Ed Pulaski, a U.S. Forest Service ranger, helps develop the Pulaski tool, still used today in firefighting.

Wisconsin

YELLOWSTONE NATIONAL PARK

NATIONAL PARK SERVICE

# Firefighting Machines

Firefighters use a variety of machines to battle flames. Fire engines are big trucks that can carry up to 3,000 gallons (11,356 liters) of water that firefighters can spray directly onto the flames. Airplanes and helicopters fly over wildfires and dump water and chemicals called fire retardants. These chemicals slow down the fire and reduce its strength, so that firefighters on the ground can put out the flames.

**1939**
The U.S. Forest Service creates a special team of firefighters, called smokejumpers, who are trained to put out fires in remote areas.

**1955**
An aircraft is used for the first time to drop water on a wildfire at Mendocino National Forest in California.

**1967**
The U.S. National Park Service allows the use of controlled fires on its land.

**2018**
California's deadliest wildfire kills 85 people and destroys nearly 19,000 buildings.

Scientists at the Missoula Fire Sciences Laboratory study fire in a wind tunnel.

# Wildfire Watch

To fight wildfires, firefighters need to know how flames behave and how that behavior changes under different conditions. To study this, researchers re-create wildfires in labs using special equipment. For example, the Missoula Fire Sciences Laboratory in Montana has a machine called a wind tunnel. Scientists can use this machine to adjust things such as temperature and wind speed. This allows them to study how wildfires spread.

# Meet a Smokejumper!

The U.S. Forest Service has a special team of firefighters called smokejumpers. These firefighters fly to remote areas and use parachutes to land near fires. Madison Whittemore is a smokejumper from Montana.

**Q.** How do smokejumpers fight wildfires?
**A.** Our goal is to put fires out before they become large. Once we get on the ground, we start digging a line around the fire. We dig deep enough to remove burnable material. With a chain saw, we can cut brush or low limbs on trees, so the fire doesn't climb up.

**Q.** How long do smokejumpers stay out in the wild?
**A.** We jump with enough food and water to last for about three days. We can always call the plane to come back and parachute in more food. Sometimes, if there's bad weather and the plane can't come, we'll have to go fishing or find food like berries. We sleep in tents in an area that's safe and not likely to burn.

**Q.** What is something unexpected that's happened on the job?
**A.** One time in the Tobacco Root Mountains in Montana, we didn't have cell service and we got a foot of snow overnight without knowing it was coming. We couldn't even find the fire the next morning!

**Q.** What is one thing you love about your job?
**A.** The people I get to work with. We all love the sense of adventure, and we appreciate how lucky we are to do what we do. We get to help serve the public and take care of public land.

Scientists collect data about the weather to predict where fires will spread. Knowing this information helps keep people safe.

**Union County Parks Fire Risk Indicator**

SMOKEY

TODAY'S FIRE DANGER

EXTREME · LOW · HIGH · MODERATE

Remember...
Only You Can Prevent Wildfires!

**FIRE CONDITIONS**
HIGH          No Campfires
EXTREME    No Fires of any kind

This sign outside a park in New Jersey warns visitors of the risk of wildfires and reminds them not to start a fire of any kind.

# Wildfire Safety

Though we often hear about wildfires burning throughout the western United States, wildfires can happen anywhere at any time. In 2019, there were wildfires in every U.S. state. But there are things you and your family can do to protect yourself and your home in case a wildfire threatens your community. You can even play a role in preventing wildfires from starting!

# Watch That Fire!

Is there anything as yummy as eating s'mores around a campfire? Whether in your backyard or out in a park, you and your family should follow certain rules for building a safe fire. Unless you can use an existing firepit, pick a spot that's at least 15 feet (5 meters) away from trees and shrubs. Make sure it's not too windy. When you're done, put out the fire with water or by covering it with dirt.

In 2017, campfires caused 111 wildfires in California.

Whether building a campfire or using a firepit like this one, it's important to keep your fire small.

# Fireproof Home

Embers blowing from a wildfire can set fire to buildings up to 1 mile (1.6 km) away. Here are a few things you and your family can do to keep your house safe in case of a wildfire.

**Gutters:** Keep gutters clean of anything that can catch fire, such as leaves.

**Trees and Plants:** Make sure bushes and trees are at least 5 feet (1.5 m) from your house.

**Building Materials:** Make sure roof, sidings, and fences are made of metal or stone, not wood.

**Yard:** Keep the backyard clean of debris.

From 2017 to 2019, about 1.1 million people were ordered to evacuate in California because of 11 large wildfires.

**A family gets ready to evacuate their home as a nearby wildfire approaches their neighborhood in South Carolina.**

## Be Ready!

Even if you don't live in an area that's at high risk for wildfires, you and your family should have a plan for what to do in case one happens. For example, you should know your **evacuation** route. That's the path you and your family can take to leave an area and get to safety. If a wildfire is nearby and emergency officials tell you to evacuate, you should do so immediately.

# Make a Go Bag!

No matter where you live, you can be affected by natural disasters. That's why it's a good idea to have a go bag packed and ready to go. What goes inside depends on you and your family. But here are a few items you don't want to forget:

- Water
- Packaged food (such as dried fruit or peanut butter)
- Cash and important documents
- Prescription medications
- Toothbrushes and toothpaste

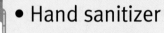

- Hand sanitizer
- Flashlights and batteries
- Radio
- Masks to protect you from smoke
- Pet supplies (if you have a pet)

# After a Fire

If you and your family have had to evacuate, you should go back to your home only after officials say it's safe to do so. Once you return home, you should wear a protective mask over your nose and mouth. It will keep you from breathing ash and other particles in the air. Also, pay attention to where you walk. Embers may be buried underground and can burn you—or even spark another fire.

A family comes back to their neighborhood to see the destruction caused after a wildfire in Oregon.

## Forces of Nature

Wildfires are some of the most destructive natural disasters in the world. They affect millions of people every year. As climate change continues, the risk of strong, large wildfires will continue to increase. But maybe you'll be part of the solution. You could become a firefighter, work to slow down climate change, or even just be extra careful next time your family has a campfire. Each of us can make a difference when it comes to wildfires!

# Fire Country

**Different factors affect whether an area is at high or low risk for wildfires.** One factor is the type of vegetation. Another is the area's **climate**, or average weather. This map shows which states in the United States have the lowest and highest potential for wildfires, based on past fires, climate, and plant life. Study the map, and then answer the questions below.

## Analyze It!

1 What is the risk for wildfires in the state of Michigan?

2 Are wildfires more likely to happen in Texas or Virginia?

3 True or False: South Carolina has low potential for wildfires.

4 What trends, or patterns, do you see in the map?

# Potential for Wildfires Across the United States

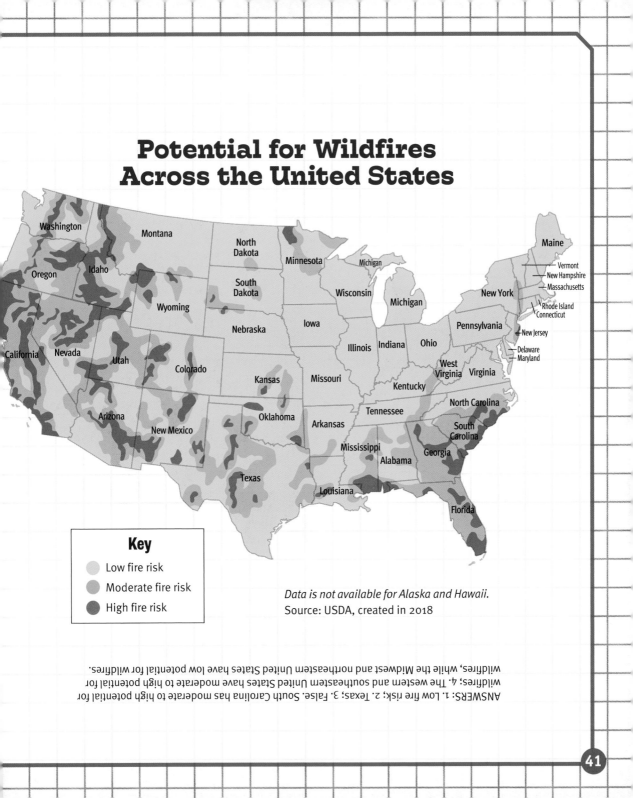

**Key**
- Low fire risk
- Moderate fire risk
- High fire risk

*Data is not available for Alaska and Hawaii.*
Source: USDA, created in 2018

ANSWERS: 1. Low fire risk; 2. Texas; 3. False. South Carolina has moderate to high potential for wildfires; 4. The western and southeastern United States have moderate to high potential for wildfires, while the Midwest and northeastern United States have low potential for wildfires.

# Sliding Land

As you learned on page 12, areas affected by wildfires are at higher risk for landslides. That's because those areas have lost the plant roots that help hold soil in place. In this activity, you will model how rain affects a wooded hill compared with a hill stripped of trees.

## Directions

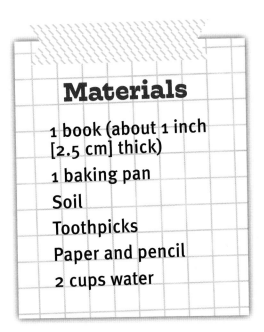

## Materials

1 book (about 1 inch [2.5 cm] thick)

1 baking pan

Soil

Toothpicks

Paper and pencil

2 cups water

**1** Prop the book under one end of the baking pan. Pack soil on the pan's raised end to create a slope that stops halfway down the pan. Add toothpicks all over your hillside, pushing them into the soil. The toothpicks represent trees. Make a drawing of your wooded hill.

**2** Slowly pour 1 cup of water down the slope. The water represents heavy rain. What happens to the soil? What about the toothpicks? Make a drawing of how the hill looks after the rain.

**3** Repeat step 1 using new soil, but this time don't add toothpicks. This slope represents a bare hillside that has lost all its trees due to a wildfire.

**4** Slowly pour 1 cup of water down the slope. What happens to the soil this time? Make a drawing and compare it to the drawing you made in step 2.

# Explain It!

**Using what you learned in this book, can you explain what happened and why? Then think: Are toothpicks a good model for trees? How are toothpicks similar to and different from real trees?**

# True Statistics

**Percentage of wildfires in the United States caused by humans in 2019:** 87 percent

**Number of wildfires in the United States started by lightning between 1992 and 2012:** 245,446

**Year the first fire engine was purchased in the United States:** 1678 in Boston, Massachusetts

**Number of wildfires in California unintentionally started by children in 2017:** 43

**Number of controlled fires started by U.S. state and federal officials in 2019:** 181,542

**Year the first woman joined the smokejumpers team:** 1981, Deanne Shulman

**Year the first women became firefighters in the United States:** 1815

**Maximum weight of gear a wildland firefighter carries:** 45 pounds (20 kg)

## Did you find the truth?

 Some tree species need wildfires to survive.

 Most wildfires in the United States are caused by lightning.

# Resources

## Other books in this series:

## You can also look at:

Claybourne, Anna. *100 Most Destructive Natural Disasters Ever*. New York: Scholastic, 2014.

Murphy, Jim. *The Great Fire*. New York: Scholastic, 2010.

Nelson Maurer, Tracy. *The World's Worst Wildfires*. Oxford, United Kingdom: Capstone Press, 2019.

Philbrick, Rodman. *Wildfire*. New York: Scholastic, 2019.

Tarshis, Lauren. *I Survived: The California Wildfires, 2018*. New York: Scholastic, 2020.

# Glossary

**arson** (AHR-suhn) the crime of setting fire to property or a wilderness area with the intention of causing harm

**atmosphere** (AT-muhs-feer) the mixture of gases that surrounds a planet

**climate** (KLYE-mit) the usual weather that happens in a place

**climate change** (KLYE-mit chaynj) an increase in temperatures on Earth and shifts in global weather patterns

**droughts** (drouts) long periods without rain; droughts damage crops and cause the soil to dry out

**ecosystems** (EE-koh-sis-tuhmz) all the living things in one place and their relationships to their environment

**embers** (EM-burz) hot, glowing pieces of a fire

**evacuation** (i-VAK-yoo-ay-shun) moving away from an area or building because it is dangerous there

**fossil fuels** (FAH-suhl FYOO-uhlz) coal, oil, or natural gas, formed from the remains of prehistoric plants and animals

**greenhouse gases** (GREEN-hous gasez) gases that trap heat in a planet's atmosphere, causing average global temperatures to rise

**landslides** (LAND-slides) masses of earth and rocks that suddenly slide down a mountain or a hill

# Index

Page numbers in **bold** indicate illustrations.

# About the Author

Alessandra Potenza is a science journalist based in New York. She is originally from Rome, Italy. Alessandra loves reading books, traveling, stargazing, and geeking out about science. Visit her website at: www.alepotenza.com